PRACTICAL STEPS: OVERCOME THE HEADACHE OF RESEARCH PROPOSAL WRITING

EXPERIENCE INDEPENDENT PROFESSIONAL RESEARCH PROPOSAL WRITING

DR RENJI ISSAC

ISBN 978-1-63745-196-0

Dedicated to merciful God with thanks for making me toovercome
the tough times

Contents

CHAPTER ONE

Introduction: Research Proposal writing

Introduction

The dream of every prospective research scholar is to become a Ph.D. holder.

Some of them are seeking professional help to attain their dream.

But the genuine people attempt to make their come true from the very beginning.

A doctorate is one of the highest qualifications across the world, irrespective of

the stream. Most of them may refer from the library or took others' help and

prepare the text in the same style of the paper that they got. There must be similarities

in the content style, language used, and even in the number of lines, too.

CHAPTER TWO

Starting Point: Research Proposal writing

Starting Point

The starting point is the mind of the scholar. It may be started a decade ago or

immediately after the post-graduation. The urge or the burning desire to obtain

a Ph.D. may make them seek, ask, and search for opportunities. These are absolutely true for all genuine researchers.

At this stage, they discuss with the seniors or classmates, read research journals and

thesis both online and print version, start taking data regarding the Ph.D. universities

and seats. Before the application stage, the real beginning point is the mind of the research aspirant.

CHAPTER THREE

Subject Selection: Research Proposal writing

Subject Selection

Any topics under the concerned subject can be selected according to institution or university rules.

It can be purely topics that come under the specific department or can be interdisciplinary in nature

related to the concerned topic or department.

Generally, the topic according to the supervisors' choice will take and complete the research.

The scholar's interest is secondary in many cases. But sitting with a supervisor to talk can resolve

the issues to some extent.

Right Topic or Guidance: Research Proposal writing

Right Topic or Guidance

Advices are abundant and free of cost.

The scholar will suffer.

The best way is to inform the guide about the heart touched

topic for the research programme, if it comes under the purview of the department.

Research Proposal?.

Research Proposal?.

Every research proposal is a document to offer what the scholar wants to find out.

The proposal deals with the issues or questions that required a solution.

Normally, the research proposal covers a situation based on the information

or as the necessity to conduct a detailed to obtain a solution.

Irrespective of the scholar's intelligence and academic records the drafted

research proposal can play a major role in the programme. **The genuine researchers are**

aware of the need, to be honest. *But the sake fake researchers may copy-paste or*

depend a ghost research writer .

CHAPTER SIX

Best policy and practice ; Resarch Proposal

Best policy and practice

To be honest, is the best policy and practice of every researcher otherwise

what the knowledge they share or impart to the society has an ill effect or

substandard to misguide the growing generation.

A research proposal can be drafted many times before its final version.

Writing, rewriting, and finalization required for every proposal because

a mere first draft may lack the exact qualities required for a scientific study.

CHAPTER SEVEN

Necessity: Research Proposal writing

Necessity

The necessity of the research proposal to have an idea about the study, they wanted to do. Mainly a proposal pointed out the main ideas that come under the study and the objectives or the expected outcomes of the study. The time required to complete the study (Ph.D. programmes have the time limit fixed by the concerned bodies or universities).

The methodology planned to follow specifically in the study. Proposed geographical area, if applicable. The variables come under the study. In most cases a fully framed proposal is exceptional, it needs to be modified to become a detailed and crystal clear plan.

The proposal should be signage to find the research gap. Research Gap finding in the concerned area of knowledge to find research questions and problems. The proposal can show the researcher's skill, the output of the study, utilization of resources, tools planned to include and analytical frameworks selected, suggestions etc:

CHAPTER EIGHT

Research Gap; Research proposal writing advanced level knowledge

Research Gap

Research Gap is the diamond on the researcher's keenness and hard work.

The left or left to find the information or knowledge related to a topic by

the past researchers or study is termed as the research gap. Finding of

research gap bridges the space between the past and present studies.

A gap in the research is a constraint to get the best outcome or result in

the decision-making process or reaching in a conclusion

Research Gap is mentioned in thesis or and in scientific publications

after the literature review.

CHAPTER NINE

Genuine proposal

Genuine proposal

The invisible strong content in the research proposal is genuineness.

A research proposal must have the following content:

Content Guideline

1. Introduction

Just to introduce what the researcher interested to find

2. Scope

Exactly what the researcher planned to cover.

3. Statement of the problem

What the researcher knows and what need to know?.

4. Significance of the study

The benefit /contribution part of the study

5. Literature Review

References from the past studies on the same topic

6. Research Methodology

Contains strategy for research, population, sample, sampling technique, tools etc: will cover.

7. Hypothesis (Optional)

Testable statement to know the relationship of the variables

8. objectives

The goals of the researcher need to be attained

9.Analysis of Framework

The statical methods used for analysis for a meaningful interpretation.

10. Limitations

The constraints / uncovered areas of the study

11. References

The sources of information collected.

CHAPTER TEN

Proposal : Research Proposal writing

Proposal Length

The length of a proposal can be of a maximum of three pages including

all the contents. The too lengthy proposal is vivid and too short may lack clarity.

Style

The words can be in times new roman letters font 12 , the line spacing should be 1.5, and left alignment is required.

Headings

The main heading can be in more than new roman letters in font 12, in most cases font 14 is applicable as bold, and center alignment is applicable.

Subheadings

The subheadings can be in Times New Roman font 12 in bold letters and left alignment is applicable.

Finishing Point

Finishing Point

The genuineness costs nothing but it values more. There is no substitute for hard work,

acquiring knowledge, and imparting.

There is much value difference between the self-written plagiarism-free proposal or thesis

or even articles in terms of satisfaction, knowledge, and morality.

The degeneration of academics has a great role in pay buying ghostwritten articles,

proposals, and thesis. How those who subcontracting the highest degree of academic works can

be effective an academician or scientist?.